Tom,
Always be SURE
~ your faith.

T-

Rom 15:13

SURE

Knowing What You Believe and Why You Believe It

Tim Menser

CROSSBOOKS
PUBLISHING

CrossBooks™
A Division of LifeWay
1663 Liberty Drive
Bloomington, IN 47403
www.crossbooks.com
Phone: 1-866-879-0502

All Scripture references, unless otherwise noted, are taken from the Holy Bible, New International Version. Copyright 1973, 1978, 1984 by International Bible Society. Used by permission of Zondervan Publishing House. All rights reserved.

First published by CrossBooks 2/06/2012

ISBN: 978-1-4627-1150-5 (hc)
ISBN: 978-1-4627-1148-2 (sc)
ISBN: 978-1-4627-1149-9 (e)

Library of Congress Control Number: 2011919693

Printed in the United States of America

This book is printed on acid-free paper.

Any people depicted in stock imagery provided by Thinkstock are models, and such images are being used for illustrative purposes only.

Certain stock imagery © Thinkstock.

Because of the dynamic nature of the Internet, any web addresses or links contained in this book may have changed since publication and may no longer be valid. The views expressed in this work are solely those of the author and do not necessarily reflect the views of the publisher, and the publisher hereby disclaims any responsibility for them.

DEDICATION

First, I want to dedicate this book to Jeff Gray, who encouraged me to write. You are a great friend, Jeff. Be encouraged. God is doing great things through you.

Second, I want to dedicate this book to Elmer Langdon, a dear friend who has gone on to be with the Lord. In his lifetime, he committed himself to helping young men and women grow up in the faith.

Third, I want to dedicate this book to my friends and former students in Zambia and Malawi, as well as to those continuing to carry the good news to the ends of the earth. Remember, the enemy is always trying to lead you astray with false teachings. Know the Word of God and always be sure of what you believe.

Finally, I want to dedicate this to my family, who supported me as I worked on this book. You bless me every day with your love.

Now faith is being sure of what we hope for and certain of what we do not see. Hebrews 11:1

Now faith is being sure of what we hope for and certain of what we do not see.
Hebrews 11:1 NIV

CONTENTS

PREFACE

As I began to grow in my faith, I looked for a simple-to-understand book about what most Christians believe. Each book I found seemed to rely heavily on difficult terms and concepts. I often felt that I would never be able to know what the Bible taught on certain subjects of the faith unless I became a master of the Greek and Hebrew languages.

As I grew in my faith, I continued to search for a book I could give to new believers or to those (like myself) who had a lot of questions but were struggling to find the answers. Even though the subject seemed important to me, I was still unable to find what I was seeking.

While I was serving on the mission field in Africa, a fellow missionary told me that he was looking for a simple book about Christian doctrine. He wanted it to be easy enough for a kid to understand. When I told him I had been looking for the same thing, Jeff challenged me to write the book.

Life on the mission field made me increasingly aware of the overwhelming need for basic discipleship—not just in Africa, but in the United States as well. While in Zambia, I had the wonderful opportunity to befriend a local pastor named Henry. We would discuss doctrinal issues, and he would often reply, "Sure" (pronounced "shoo-wa" with his Zambian accent). He was *sure* about his faith. He was *sure* about the teachings of God's Word. He inspires me today as he remains committed to teaching these *sure* truths to other pastors and the members of his village and church.

As this book started coming together, I tried to cover most of the essential doctrinal (basic belief) issues. I also wanted to provide discussion questions at the end of each chapter. This book was initially intended to be for teens to help them understand why they believe what they believe. As I discussed the book with others, however, it became clear that many adults have also been seeking a straightforward approach that answers—in simple, everyday language—the questions about what we believe and why we believe it.

It is my prayer that this book will help others to be like Henry in Africa—*sure* in the faith of "what we hope for and certain of what we do not see."

ACKNOWLEDGMENTS

I would first like to thank the Lord for allowing me to walk through many experiences that have enabled me to be *sure* of my faith. Even though the journey has been difficult at times, the resulting peace and closeness I share with my Father have made me thankful for the struggles.

Next, I want to thank my wife, Jill, for reading copy after copy of the book and assisting me with grammar, organization, and at times, recollection. You are an amazing life partner. I am very glad God gave us to one another. I also want to thank my sons, Zac and Will, for reading the draft and showing me the areas that needed simplification and clarification. I want to thank my parents and my brothers, Don and Dave, for their insights and encouragement in the process—not just throughout the development of this book, but also throughout my entire life.

I want to thank Jeff Gray for telling me to write the book and believing I could do it. Your encouragement means more than you know.

Finally, I want to thank Laura Benton Elliott, who is a schoolteacher, church member, and friend. The time you took away from your work and family in order to provide the final two edits was helpful and greatly appreciated. Thank you for sharing in this work.

INTRODUCTION

FOLLOWING MY OWN WISDOM

*Now faith is being sure of what we hope for and certain
of what we do not see.*
Hebrews 11:1

I was blessed as a child. I was raised in a Christian home and was taken to a Bible-teaching church throughout my childhood. Because of my strong Christian background, the support of my parents, the coaching of my big brothers, and the counsel of a solid pastor, I asked Christ into my heart when I was seven years old. Many think seven is too young to be saved. While I didn't understand much about the finer points of theology, I knew I had sinned and needed forgiveness that could only come from Jesus if I wanted to go to heaven. I believed in God. I believed that His "only begotten Son" was Jesus. I knew Jesus died on the cross to pay for my sins. I knew that on Easter Sunday (just three days after He died), He rose from the grave, showing He was more powerful than death. Therefore, I trusted Jesus and asked Him to save me. A few weeks later, I was baptized. My spiritual journey had begun.

Unfortunately, soon after, my journey stalled. I had a Bible, but I seldom read it. It was just so big and too hard to understand. All of the *thees* and *thous* were confusing to me. So, a few years later, my parents bought me a Bible that would be easier to understand and written in modern English. However, it still seemed like it was too much to piece together. I prayed, but my prayers were generally the same night after night. I wasn't growing in my faith or in my relationship with Jesus.

As I grew older, I became involved in more and more things that were outside the will of God. I knew these behaviors were not pleasing to the Lord, but I figured He'd understand. I believed He had saved me; therefore, I would go to heaven no matter what I did. I came to the conclusion that God was very interested in whether people went to heaven or hell, and He left the rest up to us. It was my life, and I was going to live it.

The more I progressed in school, the more I became exposed to the world's teachings. The Bible describes the world's teachings as contrary to the Word of God. More specifically, worldly wisdom is a system of ideas and thinking which has a purpose of denying the truths set forth in Scripture. For example, in science classes, I learned that evolution was the key to the beginnings of life on the planet. In church, I learned that God created everything. Since science was proven (or so I thought), I believed in science and decided the Bible was wrong on that issue. I thought the truth just wasn't known way back when the Bible was written.

I continued to rely on my own wisdom and the world's teaching. I became more and more dependent upon myself. I knew very little of God's Word. I wasn't aware that the Bible says, "Where is the wise man? Where is the scholar? Where is the philosopher of this age? Has not God made foolish the wisdom of the world?" (I Corinthians 1:20). Further, the Bible says that "the foolishness of God is wiser than man's wisdom, and the weakness of God is stronger than man's strength" (I Corinthians 1:25). In other words, my wisdom was coming from a system that had a set purpose of opposing God's Word. My wisdom, while it seemed wise to me, did not come close to the wisdom of God.

My own wisdom seemed to be working well for me until I was about eighteen years old. During my freshman year of college, I began to see the holes in my way of thinking. Things didn't always work out the way I wanted. Some situations were beyond my control. The first major event occurred a few years earlier, and it later proved disastrous. Both of my older brothers got married, joined the Navy, and moved away. I missed them, but there was much more at stake than I realized. A rather large piece of my support system had been taken away from me, and I didn't even realize it.

Once I was in college, other problems began to take shape. I was involved in a relationship with my high school sweetheart. We had been together (off and on) for a long time. Everyone (including me) assumed we would eventually get married. One evening, toward the end of my freshman year, she called and ended our relationship. "There is someone else," she said. I thought my heart was going to break in two. Just a few weeks later, I received another call telling me that one of my best friends had died. Then I quickly became involved in another romantic relationship and was engaged within just a few short months. Soon after our engagement was announced, I discovered my fiancé was not being faithful to me. The losses were really beginning to mount.

The problem wasn't the fact that I went through some significant losses. We all go through losses. We all face times of a broken heart. In fact, the Bible tells us that bad things are going to happen. Jesus said, "In this world you will have trouble. But take heart! I have overcome the world" (John 16:33, NIV). The problem was that I had bought into the world's system rather than trusting in God to walk with me and take care of me.

As I tried to deal with my problems, my sinful behavior continued to increase. I was trying to do anything I could to deal with the pain in my life. During a particularly difficult night, I heard the words of a song by the Christian singer Carmen. The chorus of "Fear Not, My Child" reminded me that I should not be afraid because the Lord was with me during both the good and difficult times.

For the first time in my life, I realized God wanted more for me than to rescue me from hell. He wanted to walk with me every day of my life. He wanted me to know Him and to trust Him. I remember praying something like this: "God, if this really is who you are, I want to know you like that. I want to know you care for me and are concerned about my problems. I want to know I am not alone because you are walking with me."

So I went to church. Yet there was a problem. Most of the churches I visited didn't have the answers for which I was looking and didn't seem to like the fact that I was asking hard questions about the faith. I just kept looking. I wanted to really know God. I wanted *truth*. I finally landed at Living Hope Baptist Church in Bowling Green, Kentucky. The believers there didn't always have the answers for my questions, either; yet they took time, listened, and opened the Bible with me to help find the answers.

After several weeks of asking and listening, I recommitted my life to Jesus Christ. I thanked God for being patient with me. I thanked Him again for forgiving me of my sins. From that day forward, I would seek to follow Him wherever He wanted me to go and do whatever He wanted me to do. I asked God to take control of my life. From that time, He began to heal the wounds in my heart. He encouraged my spirit and gave me a renewed sense of purpose in my life. He brought joy into my life that went beyond my daily circumstances. He made me *sure* for the first time that I was never alone. He made me *sure* that I could trust in Him and His Word.

The following pages tell the findings of my spiritual journey. I cannot say all of this information came to me right away. God has continued even to this day to challenge my thoughts, beliefs, and level of commitment. I continue to learn more about His love and how to trust Him fully. I pray you will carefully examine the truth of God's Word and travel with God as well—to be *sure*.

CHAPTER 1

THE BIBLE

THE BIBLE

When I was a college student, I had a friend who had a problem with the truth. It's not that he had a problem hearing the truth; he had a problem telling the truth. That's a nice way of saying he was a liar. He was always making up stories, so others would be impressed with him. Since he told the truth only part of the time, I was not able to believe him any of the time. I never trusted him.

I had a similar problem with the Bible. Some people, such as a few of my teachers and friends, claimed that the information in the Bible about creation and miracles just simply wasn't true. My trust in the Bible as God's Word began to decline as I trusted more in what my teachers and others said than the Bible. I was confused by what they said, but I thought I couldn't argue with science.

I had a second problem with the Bible when I was in college. I had never really read it! Of course I had read parts—small parts—but not the whole thing and not in context with what the rest of the Bible said. It also felt so big and too complicated. I could never get through it or really understand it. I depended upon others to tell me what the Bible said and what it meant.

After the difficult season in my life, I felt I needed to make a decision. I needed to trust God's Word or reject it as simply a collection of stories from the past. During this period, I investigated the Bible and discovered some important facts. I learned that the Old Testament features over three hundred prophecies written about Jesus, and He fulfilled every single one of them. These prophecies were written years before He was born. I also learned that even though over forty different people from thirteen different countries and three continents wrote the Bible, it has perfect unity, is without contradictions, and points toward the common theme of God's plan to save us because of His love. The more I studied, the more I discovered that the Bible doesn't contradict science—it contradicts the opinions of certain scientists! Some scientists actually agree with the Bible's account of creation. After discovering these facts, I decided to trust the Bible. Sometimes I don't understand it, but I trust it as God's Word.

KEY THEOLOGY

The Bible is God's Word. Every word of it is the truth. He gave it to us to help us discover how to learn more about Him, how to love Him more, and how to love one another. Reading the Bible will help us grow strong in our faith. Here's what the Bible says about itself: "All Scripture is God-breathed and is useful for teaching, rebuking, correcting and training in righteousness, so that the man of God may be thoroughly equipped for every good work" (II Timothy 3:16-17).

As you read earlier, many different people wrote the Bible over a long period of time. God filled each author with His Holy Spirit so they would write His exact message for His people.

The Bible has two major divisions, the Old Testament and the New Testament. The Old Testament teaches us about the beginning of all things, that sin became a problem, and about the old covenant (or promise) of how God would relate to people. It is also filled with prophecy about Jesus coming to earth in order to take away our guilt and sin and fill us with hope and joy. The New Testament teaches us about the coming of Jesus. It is filled with His miracles and His teachings. It also teaches us about the establishment of the New Testament church, how to live for Jesus, and about the future return of Jesus.

Both the New Testament and the Old Testament are important to us, so we can understand God's plan. The message of the Bible is that our sin separates us from a relationship with God. It tells us what God has done in order to restore our relationship with Him. The Bible teaches us how great God is and how much He values and loves us.

KEY TRUTH

The Bible is God's Word, and all of it is true and helpful.

KEY VERSE

"For the word of God is living and active. Sharper than any double-edged sword, it penetrates even to dividing soul and spirit, joints and marrow; it judges the thoughts and attitudes of the heart" (Hebrews 4:12).

KEY QUESTIONS

What do you believe about the Bible? Why do you believe it?

How does your belief about the Bible affect the way you live your life?

Do you think it is important to read and study the Bible?
Why or why not?

What does it mean when the Bible says that "all Scripture is God-breathed" (II Timothy 3:16)?

In what way is the Bible "living and active" (Hebrews 4:12)?

If you struggle with understanding the Bible, what are some things you could do to improve your understanding?

- Get an easier translation such as the New International Version, Holman Christian Standard Version, New Living Translation, or New King James Version
- Have a Bible teacher or Christian friend help you
- Talk to a pastor
- Buy a book (Bible commentary) to help you such as Warren Wiersbe's *Be* Series

What step are you going to take to grow in your trust and understanding of God's Word?

Draw a picture demonstrating Hebrews 4:12.

CHAPTER 2

GOD

GOD

I used to believe God was distant. He was up in heaven, looking down, and checking on me. I believed He was very interested in saving me, so I could go to heaven instead of hell. That was it. I thought He more or less left the rest of my life up to me.

As a college student, I made several bad decisions and realized I needed help. My life was not going the way I wanted! During that difficult time, I realized God had always wanted to help. He wanted to walk with me throughout my life. He was just waiting for me to ask Him to take control.

KEY THEOLOGY

Who is God? God has always existed. He is the most powerful being that has ever existed. God is omnipotent meaning nothing—or no one—is greater or stronger than Him. He is omniscient meaning He knows everything. He is omnipresent meaning He is everywhere at the same time. He created everything in the world (including you). He loves you and wants you to know Him. It may sound strange, but God wants to be in a relationship with you.

Even though God is one God, He exists in three persons: the Father, the Son, and the Holy Spirit. *Person*, in this case, does not mean that God is a human being. *Person* rather refers to the fact that God exists as different identities within His being. Now, here's the hard-to-understand part. Each person of God (the Father, Son, and Holy Spirit) exists as a specific identity. Each has His own role in the world, but all come together as one God. While Jesus was on earth, He prayed to His Father in heaven and promised the coming of the Holy Spirit. However, He is not three gods. He is one.

We find evidence of God being three in one throughout the Bible. For example, "Then God said, 'Let us make man in our image, in our likeness'" (Genesis 1:26). Did you catch the plural pronoun? "Let *us* make man in *our* image." This is the Father, the Son, and the Holy Spirit working together in creation. However, we also find that God is one God. "The Lord our God, the Lord is one" (Deuteronomy 6:4). He is one God consisting of three persons: the Father, the Son, and the Holy Spirit.

Are you confused yet? Don't worry. Many, including myself, have been confused about this issue for years. The problem occurs when we compare God to things we see here on earth. When we do that, we commit heresy. Heresy is an opinion that contradicts biblical truth. For example, some compare the Trinity to water, steam, and ice. Each has the same elemental components but can change states as needed. The problem with this description is when water becomes steam it ceases to be water. It becomes something else. This illustration is a heresy called *modalism*. Modalism teaches that God ceases to exist as Father in order to become the Son. He ceases to be the Son in order to become the Holy Spirit. The Bible teaches that while Jesus was on earth, He prayed to the Father. He also promised the coming of the Holy Spirit. All three, the Father, the Son, and the Holy Spirit, existed at the same time, and continue to exist together today.

There are other incorrect theories using earthly examples to describe God. Some people try to compare the Trinity to the roles of a man. A man can be a husband, a businessman, and a father. He is one person with different roles. This comparison, too, is heresy because the man is still one man, not three men. The truth is that you cannot compare the Trinity to any created thing on earth. There is nothing on earth like God. It is impossible to fully explain God using human wisdom. Faith is required. We must trust God is who He says He is. We come to know Him through faith, and He blesses us.

KEY TRUTH

There is only one true God. He exists in three persons: the Father, the Son, and the Holy Spirit.

KEY VERSE

"Hear, O Israel: The Lord our God, the Lord is one" (Deuteronomy 6:4).

KEY QUESTIONS

Does God ever feel far away from you?

List a few times in your life when God felt close.

List a few times in your life when He felt far away.

What do you think made the difference in your feelings?

Does the Bible teach God is far or God is near?

What are some characteristics of God, which might affect how you feel about Him?

Are you confused or comforted by the fact there is nothing on earth that compares with God? Why?

Do you know more about the Father, the Son, or the Holy Spirit?

Are you afraid of the Father, the Son, or the Holy Spirit? Do you trust one more than the others? Why or why not?

CHAPTER 3

GOD THE FATHER

GOD THE FATHER

I love to think of God as Father. When I was a kid, I thought my father was the strongest man in the world. I always felt safe when he was around. Sometimes I woke up during the night, thinking I had heard a noise. I could overcome my fear quickly because I believed my dad could take care of anyone who might try to break in and harm us. Now that I am a father, I know I'm no match for an intruder. However, I know God the Father is all-powerful, and He promises to take care of those who belong to Him. Over and over again in the Bible, God tells us not to fear because He is with us.

God the Father not only protects us, but also disciplines us so we will grow to be mature in our faith. God meets our needs and cares for us in every way. According to the Bible, He even loves to give us good gifts (Matthew 7:11).

I know some may not be able to relate to God as Father because they did not have good experiences with their fathers. Perhaps your father left when you were young. Perhaps he died or you never knew him. Maybe your father has hurt you in some way. God wants you to know He isn't like that. He promises to never leave you and always protect you.

KEY THEOLOGY

God the Father is love. He loves us in a perfect way. He wants everyone to love Him and become His children. The Bible clearly says we can depend on God and His love, because "God is love" (I John 4:16). Did you get that? God not only knows *how* to love, but He also *is* love (I John 4:8, 16).

God is also *just*. *Just* means that right things are rewarded and wrong things are punished. The Bible teaches "all His ways are just"

(Deuteronomy 32:4). God has to punish us when we sin because He loves us. He wants us to be obedient, so we can enjoy the good things He wants to give us. No one likes to think about being punished. Yet punishment can be a good thing if it is carried out correctly and in love. When we are punished, we are taught right from wrong. The punishment itself serves as a reminder that there are consequences for our sin.

God is also full of mercy and grace. God's mercy means that we do not get what we deserve—eternal punishment and separation from God. God's grace means that we *get* something that we do not deserve—an eternity in heaven with Him. Without God's mercy, we would be in serious trouble. Therefore, He provided forgiveness for us through His Son, Jesus. Grace takes God's goodness even a step further. Because of His grace, He makes *us* His sons and daughters and gives us the promise of His kingdom in heaven.

KEY TRUTH

God is a loving Father who desires to protect us, give us good gifts, and discipline us. He desires to be intimately involved in our lives, so we do not go down the wrong path.

KEY VERSE

"How great is the love the Father has lavished on us, that we should be called children of God! And that is what we are!" (I John 3:1a)

KEY QUESTIONS

How does it feel to know that if you belong to God, you are a child of the Creator of the universe and the King of Kings?

Are you comforted or frightened when you think of God as Father?

Is there a verse in the Bible about God as Father that brings you comfort?

What is a "good gift" that God the Father has given you?

What does it mean when people say "God is a just God"?

How do God's grace and mercy help us?

CHAPTER 4

GOD THE SON—JESUS

GOD THE SON—JESUS

Jesus was the part of the faith I always thought I understood—until I really thought about Him. I knew the Christmas stories about His birth. I also knew the Easter stories about His resurrection. I knew that Jesus died on the cross to pay for my sins and if I believed in Him, I would go to heaven. It seemed simple enough until I asked the questions "how" and "why." Why would Jesus suffer a terrible and painful death for someone like me? How could He love me that much? *He doesn't even know me,* I thought. That is when I realized how wrong I was. He *does* know me. He sees my sin. He understands my thoughts and my heart. These facts are true about Jesus, because He is not just the Son of God—He *is* God.

KEY THEOLOGY

Jesus is the Son of God. He calls God His Father. Many think that Jesus did not exist until He was born in Bethlehem to Mary and Joseph; however, the Bible teaches He has always existed. Jesus says He is the "Alpha and the Omega" (Revelation 22:3). *Alpha* is the first letter of the Greek alphabet, and *omega* is the last. Jesus was saying He is the beginning and the end. Jesus was actively involved in creation, as described in John 1. He was *the Word* being spoken—bringing everything into being. In the book of Revelation, we find Jesus returning to restore justice and saving those who belong to Him from the coming destruction. He has always lived and will always live. He is God.

Jesus' birth was a miracle. He was born of a virgin (Matthew 1:18). He lived a perfect life and never sinned (II Corinthians 5:21). He taught many wonderful things about God the Father and what His kingdom is like. Many people did not want to hear Jesus' teachings, so the Jewish leaders had Him arrested and put to death by the Roman authorities (Matthew 26:3-5). The Roman authorities nailed Him to a cross (Matthew 27:27-56). After He was confirmed to be dead, His body was removed from the cross, placed in a tomb, and sealed with a stone (John 19:33-42). Roman guards were even placed in front of the tomb in order to keep anyone from stealing Jesus' body (Matthew 27:62-66). However, on the third day after His death, the earth shook, and the stone rolled away. The tomb was empty. Jesus had risen from the dead! He later met with His followers and told them to tell everyone about Him, His love, and His power (Matthew 28:1-20). Jesus then returned to heaven. He promises that someday, He will come again to destroy all evil and take us home to be with the Father forever (Acts 1:6-11).

KEY TRUTH

Jesus is God's Son. He died for our sins and rose from the dead on Easter Sunday.

KEY VERSE

"The Son is the radiance of God's glory and the exact representation of his being, sustaining all things by his powerful word. After he had provided purification for sins, he sat down at the right hand of the Majesty in heaven" (Hebrews 1:3).

KEY QUESTIONS

If Jesus is the Son of God, how can we also say He is God?

What does it mean that Jesus was without sin?

How did Jesus show His love for you?

How can you show your love for Jesus?

How does it make you feel to know that Jesus is coming again to take His followers to heaven?

CHAPTER 5

GOD THE HOLY SPIRIT

GOD THE HOLY SPIRIT

The Holy Spirit is a subject of much controversy in our churches. The main reason for the controversy, I believe, is we are afraid of Him. I was afraid of Him. I realized that if the Holy Spirit took control of my life, then *I* would be out of control. I wanted to be in control of my own life. *What if He causes me to do something embarrassing?* I thought. I definitely didn't want to be called a "Holy Roller" or have people think I was some kind of religious nut! Therefore, I tried to keep Him at arm's length—just enough distance away so I could stay in control. Later, through God's Word, I learned that God did not send His Holy Spirit to cause problems in my life; rather, He sent His Holy Spirit to solve problems in my life. The first thing I had to do was to trust Him and allow Him to take control. I had to know the identity of the Holy Spirit.

KEY THEOLOGY

The Holy Spirit is God. Like God the Father and God the Son, He has existed from the beginning. The Holy Spirit is a *person,* not an *it.* He is the third person of the Trinity. We first see the Holy Spirit at work in Genesis 1:2 as "the Spirit of God [that] was hovering over the waters." As God the Father created, the Holy Spirit sustained the creation. He spoke the inspired words that were written in the Bible. He tells our hearts and minds when we sin against God—He convicts us. The Holy Spirit loves us and draws us toward a relationship with God. When we belong to God, the Holy Spirit lives in our hearts to teach us, encourage us, and help us become more like God. In John 14, Jesus teaches His disciples that He will soon be put to death. He tells them He will not leave them to be alone, though. He explains that He will send "another Counselor to be with you forever—the Spirit of truth" (John 14:16-17).

The Holy Spirit also gives us special gifts (abilities), so we can do great things for God while we are here on the earth. Examples of these gifts include teaching, helping, and sharing God's love with others. God wants to use you—no matter your age, race, or gender—to do great things for Him.

KEY TRUTH

The Holy Spirit is not an *it;* He is a person. He is God. The Holy Spirit convicts the world of sin. He lives in the life of a believer in order to provide help and encouragement. If we cooperate with the Holy Spirit, He will assist us in doing great things for God and His kingdom.

KEY VERSE

"Do you not know that your body is a temple of the Holy Spirit, who is in you, whom you have received from God? You are not your own; you were bought at a price. Therefore honor God with your body" (I Corinthians 6:19-20).

KEY QUESTIONS

Why does it matter if we call the Holy Spirit *it* rather than *He*?

How is the work of God the Holy Spirit different from the work of God the Son, Jesus?

Is it frightening to you to allow the Holy Spirit to be in control of your life? Why or why not?

What are some gifts that you believe the Holy Spirit has given to you (such as teaching, helping others, encouraging, leadership, etc.)?

What does the phrase "you were bought at a price" in I Corinthians 6:19-20 mean to you?

In what ways are you cooperating with the Holy Spirit in your own life?

In what ways are you not cooperating with the Holy Spirit in your own life?

CHAPTER 6

HUMANITY

HUMANITY

God created the earth, plants, animals, and everything else in the world—the entire universe. After each creative act, God proclaimed what He created was good. God loves everything He made—especially people. When God made people, He said they were very good. God created people in order to have a relationship with them.

You need to know you are special. God loves you, and He wants to spend time with you. The very reason He made you was to love you. However, everyone, at different times, feels unloved or even unlovable.

There was a time in my life when I experienced several losses in a short period of time. My older brothers got married and moved far away. I went through a bad break-up, a close friend was killed, and I felt distanced from some other close friends. I felt very isolated. The enemy, Satan, began trying to convince me no one cared—that I was alone. That's what the enemy does. He wants you to think you are worthless and you cannot be loved. But God says He loves you. In fact, the Bible says, "I am convinced that neither death nor life, neither angels nor demons, neither the present nor the future, nor any powers, neither height nor depth, nor anything else in all creation, will be able to separate us from the love of God that is in Christ Jesus our Lord" (Romans 8:38-39).

KEY THEOLOGY

People are God's special creation. We are made in God's image as men and women, boys and girls. God made us male and female according to His special purposes. Since God made all people, it's natural that He loves them. He wants to be in a relationship with them. Also, all people deserve to be respected and treated in a way that would be pleasing to God.

When God first created people, they were without sin. But, as we read in the beginning of the Bible (Genesis 3), Adam and Eve—the first two people God created—were tempted and *chose* to disobey God. Because of that first sin, humanity lost its innocence, and future generations inherited hearts drawn to sin.

KEY TRUTH

God created all people in His image in order to have a relationship with them.

KEY VERSE

"So God created man in his own image, in the image of God he created him; male and female he created them" (Genesis 1:27).

KEY QUESTIONS

How can you know God loves you?

What does it mean to be created in the image of God?

If all people are created in the image of God, how should we treat others?

Have you ever had a time when you felt alone or unloved? What does God's Word teach us about this feeling?

Why does the enemy try to make us feel unloved?

How can you help others understand how much God loves them?

CHAPTER 7

Sin

SIN

Sin sounds like such a harsh word. We would like to think only bad people sin, but that simply is not true. Even the apostle Paul, who wrote several books in the New Testament, sinned. Paul talked about his struggle with sin in Romans 7:14-25. Basically, he said that often he ended up doing things he knew he shouldn't do, and he failed to do the things he knew he should do. He even referred to himself as a "wretched man" (Romans 7:24).

Many people believe there is no such thing as right and wrong. According to them, something that is wrong to you may be right for me. The world wants you to feel good about yourself by convincing you that you do not sin. Rather, sometimes you simply make bad choices. This idea is contrary to God's Word. In fact, the Bible teaches that everyone sins. Romans 3:23 states, "all have sinned and fall short of the glory of God." God wants you to feel good about yourself, too. However, He wants you to feel even better because you know the truth about yourself, and you have let Him get rid of the sin in your life.

The word *sin* means "to miss the mark." Imagine you are shooting an arrow at a target. The mark is the center—the bull's eye—perfect. We sin any time we miss the mark—any time we fail to be in the perfect center of God's plan. We sin when we do bad things. We even sin when we only do part of what God wants us to do. We sin when we do good things with the wrong motive.

The problem is that sin separates us from God. Isaiah writes, "your iniquities (sins) have separated you from your God; your sins have hidden His face from you, so that He will not hear" (Isaiah 59:2). Now remember from the previous chapter how much God loves you—even when you sin. Even though sin impacts your close relationship with Him, nothing can separate you from the *love* of God.

KEY THEOLOGY

What is sin? Sin is any behavior displeasing to God. Some people think sin is simply breaking one of the Ten Commandments. Sin also includes the times God tells us to do good things, but we do not do them. Because God is perfect (He has *never* sinned), our sins separate us from God—sort of like land divided by a river with no bridge. Imagine yourself standing on the edge of a large river valley. Now, picture God on the other side of the valley. The river valley separating you from God is your sin. No matter how hard you try, you cannot overcome the river valley on your own. The valley is too deep and the distance is too wide. You are separated from God by your sins. The problem is no matter how many good things we try to do, we can never make up for the sins we have committed. God provided a way for us to be forgiven of our sins and have a restored relationship with Him. It's like God built a bridge over the river, so we could get to Him. When we trust in Jesus' sacrifice to pay for our sins, our relationship with God can be restored. Jesus is our bridge to God.

KEY TRUTH

Sin is any behavior displeasing to God.

KEY VERSE

"Everyone who sins breaks the law; in fact, sin is lawlessness" (I John 3:3).

KEY QUESTIONS

Is it possible to live your entire life without sinning?

What is sin?

Have you ever sinned?

According to the Bible, how does our sin affect our relationship with God?

Why does the world want to convince you that you do not sin?

Why would Satan want to convince you that you have never sinned?

How does God deal with our sin?

Draw a sketch of yourself separated from God by your sin. You can use the idea of the river valley presented in the Key Theology section as a suggestion. After you complete your sketch, add a sketch illustrating how God provided a way to overcome your sin through Jesus.

CHAPTER 8

Salvation

SALVATION

What does it mean to be lost? How do we get saved? Some people think getting saved means to start being good. Others think it means to join a church or to be baptized. While it is important for us to try to be obedient, go to church, and be baptized, these works will not save us. These actions cannot save us because they will not get rid of all of the bad things we've already done.

KEY THEOLOGY

The Bad News

The Bible teaches that all of us have sinned. "For all have sinned and fall short of the glory of God" (Romans 3:23). The Bible also teaches that because of our sin, we have earned death. "The wages of sin is death" (Romans 6:23a).

A *wage* is something you earn. Think of it in terms of a job. When you work, you expect to be paid for the work you have done. You earn your wages by performing the required work. Likewise, when we sin, we earn something—a wage—and the wage is death. Death is what we deserve because of our sin. That's the bad news. However, the verse doesn't end there. It ends with *good news*.

The Good News

The rest of Romans 6:23 says, "but the gift of God is eternal life in Christ Jesus our Lord." A gift is *not* something you earn. A gift is something someone gives you because he or she loves you. God loves you! He loves you so much He gave His only Son, Jesus, to die on the cross in order to pay for your sins. "For God so loved the world that he gave his one and only Son, that whoever believes in him shall not perish but have eternal life" (John 3:16).

God promises to let Jesus' death on the cross count as our punishment for our sins. That's incredible! Why did God do that? He did it because He knew the punishment was more than we could bear. He also knew that because Jesus is God, He is more powerful than death. He knew Jesus would defeat death when He rose from the dead! He also knew Jesus' victory over death would give *us* victory over death as well, which means we will continue to live in heaven even after we die.

The Good News Gets Better

We do not have to complete a series of tasks in order to gain God's forgiveness. We only have to trust in what Jesus did for us on the cross. "For all who call on the name of the Lord will be saved" (Romans 10:13).

Trusting Jesus means we agree that God's Word is true—we have sinned. Next, we believe Jesus is who the Bible says He is and He died for us on the cross. Then, we ask God to forgive us and to send His Holy Spirit to come and live in our hearts. Finally, we follow the Holy Spirit by obeying God's Word and doing what He tells us to do.

Following Christ means we are repenting. To *repent* means to turn away from the direction we are going and begin to go in a new direction. When we commit to follow Christ, we are saying we are no longer going to go our own way; we are going to follow Christ and do what He wants us to do.

We do not repent in order to *earn* God's love or forgiveness; we repent because we love God, and we *want* to do the things that please Him. It is not possible to be saved without repenting. Repentance shows we love and trust Christ. Jesus said, "If anyone loves me, he will obey my teaching" (John 14:23).

Remember, this is God's plan for your life. He loves you so much, and He wants to spend *forever* with you in heaven.

KEY TRUTH

God offers salvation to all who will receive Him. He does not want anyone to reject Him. All of us have sinned. Sin separates us from God. Because of sin, we deserve death. But God offered another way. Jesus died to pay for our sins. We do not have to earn our salvation. Jesus freely gives it to us if we will trust and follow Him.

KEY VERSES

"For all have sinned and fall short of the glory of God" (Romans 3:23).

"For the wages of sin is death, but the gift of God is eternal life in Christ Jesus our Lord" (Romans 6:23).

"For God so loved the world that he gave his one and only Son, that whoever believes in him shall not perish but have eternal life" (John 3:16).

"That if you confess with your mouth, 'Jesus is Lord,' and believe in your heart that God raised him from the dead, you will be saved" (Romans 10:10).

"Everyone who calls on the name of the Lord will be saved" (Romans 10:13).

KEY QUESTIONS

Will performing good deeds save you? Why or why not?

If you stop sinning now and you never sin again in your entire life, will that save you? Why or why not?

What is the penalty for sin?

How does Jesus' death on the cross help us?

Why would God send his Son, Jesus, to die on the cross for our sins?

What does it mean to repent?

Is it possible to be saved without repenting?

Draw a picture of your life with sin in it. Draw a second picture of your life without sin. Now illustrate yourself walking away from a specific sin or write a poem describing your life in sin and contrasting it with your life when your sins are forgiven.

If you are not saved or if you are unsure, what next step do you think you should take in order to be saved? If you are unsure of your next step, allow me to suggest a couple of ideas. First, right now you could pray and repent of your sins, asking Jesus to save you and lead you. Don't be intimidated by prayer. Prayer is simply talking to God like you would talk to a friend. There are no magical words or secret formulas. Sincerely talk to God, admit your sin, and tell Him you believe in Jesus. Tell Him you want to be forgiven and want Jesus to lead you for the rest of your life. If you are still unsure about your next step, call a leader in your church or trusted Christian friend to help you.

CHAPTER 9

HEAVEN AND HELL

HEAVEN

I love to think about heaven and imagine what it looks like. Walking, talking, and laughing with Jesus will be amazing ways to spend an afternoon. I love to think about seeing my friends and family members who have died and gone to heaven. No place on earth can compare to heaven.

The Bible tells us heaven will be beautiful. We learn we will see the prophets of old as well as loved ones—saved friends and family members who died before us. We will know them, and they will know us. In Revelation 21, John describes his vision of what heaven looks like. He describes it as a place built of beautiful materials, such as gold and costly gemstones. He says a river waters a beautiful garden. John also explains that there is no temple because a temple is not necessary. We no longer need to go to church because Jesus is there with us. The sun and moon do not shine there because Jesus provides the light for heaven and there will be no more night. In addition, some of the most exciting and comforting thoughts in this passage teach us that there will be no pain or sorrow in heaven.

KEY THEOLOGY

Jesus promised to prepare a special place for us in heaven when we begin to follow Him. You cannot earn your way to heaven; you can only go there if you have a relationship with Jesus. The Bible describes heaven as our eternal reward for trusting Jesus. Heaven is our inheritance as children of God. It is a place totally free of the influence of Satan. We will be healed of all of our earthly limitations and illnesses. We will be free from pain and sorrow.

SURE

KEY TRUTH

Heaven is a real place. God lives there, and He wants all people to go there to be with Him.

KEY VERSE

"In my Father's house are many rooms; if it were not so, I would have told you. I am going there to prepare a place for you. And if I go and prepare a place for you, I will come back and take you to be with me that you also may be where I am" (John 14:2-3).

HELL

You may be wondering, *If God loves everyone, then why is there a hell, and why do some people go there?* God provides salvation to all people, but some people refuse to accept Him. God loves all people, but He will not force people to love Him. If people choose to reject God and deny His only Son, Jesus, then they will have to pay for their own sins in hell. Remember, we have earned death and hell with our sin. God does not send us to hell; our rejection of God's grace and mercy causes us to go to hell.

Many people do not like to talk about hell. They are afraid they will offend someone. Others deny the existence of hell altogether. They say hell is really just the hard times we face here on earth. However, the Bible is clear that hell is a real place, and real people go there. Denying hell doesn't change the reality of its existence.

Hell is mentioned frequently in the Bible. Paul writes that God "will punish those who do not know God and do not obey the gospel of our Lord Jesus. They will be punished with everlasting destruction

41

and shut out from the presence of the Lord and from the majesty of His power" (II Thessalonians 1:8-9, NIV). Hell is described as a place burning with fire (Matthew 5:22, Revelation 19:20) where there will be weeping and gnashing of teeth (Matthew 24:51).

Hell certainly sounds like a scary place. That's why God doesn't want anyone to go there. If we belong to Jesus, we do not have to fear hell. We should be motivated to tell as many people as we can about Jesus, so others will not have to go there, either!

KEY THEOLOGY

God does not want anyone to go to hell. In fact, the Bible says (in referring to Jesus' return), "The Lord is not slow in keeping His promise, as some understand slowness. He is patient with you, not wanting anyone to perish, but everyone to come to repentance" (II Peter 3:9, NIV). The Lord wants everyone to go to heaven, but not everyone will.

Remember the words we read earlier in Romans 6:23 about the "wages of sin" being death? Death in that context means eternal death and suffering in hell. Hell is a real place, and the Bible describes it as a place of intense pain and suffering. In Revelation 20:14, it is called a lake of fire. According to Matthew 8:12, hell is a place of total darkness. People in hell are isolated—totally alone. They realize they were wrong and live with regret for all eternity.

God reveals Himself and His love to all people through His Holy Spirit. However, some refuse to listen. Only those who trust Christ and receive His forgiveness can escape hell and go to heaven.

KEY TRUTH

Hell is a real place, and real people go there. It is a place reserved for sinners who are unwilling to repent. It is filled with intense darkness, pain, and suffering for all eternity. God does not want anyone to go to hell.

KEY VERSE

"Then they will go away to eternal punishment, but the righteous to eternal life" (Matthew 25:46).

KEY QUESTIONS

Why do heaven and hell exist?

Do good people go to heaven and bad people go to hell?

Why would God want to save us from hell and take us to heaven?

What is one of the most exciting things about heaven?

Who are a few key people you are looking forward to seeing in heaven?

What do you think it will be like to see Jesus with your own eyes and walk with Him in heaven?

Since there is perfect healing in heaven, what part of you do you think will be different in heaven?

CHAPTER 10

JESUS IS THE ONLY WAY

JESUS IS THE ONLY WAY

A lot of people like to believe there are many paths (many ways) to get to heaven. They say it doesn't really matter what you believe—you simply have to be a good person and be sincere in your beliefs in order to go to heaven. That idea sounds appealing, but the Bible teaches something very different.

Being Good

We have already established in Chapter 8 that it is impossible to be good enough to go to heaven. We have all sinned and deserve punishment. There is no way we can be as good as God. In fact, the Bible teaches even our best is like "filthy rags" compared to God's goodness (Isaiah 64:6).

Just Be Sincere

Some suggest all religions teach basically the same thing, so it really doesn't matter what you believe as long as you are sincere. Actually, the idea that all religions teach the same thing is not true. Hindus believe there are many gods. Buddhists, on the other hand, deny the existence of God. Those religions are completely different. Muslims deny Jesus is God; however, Christians contend He is. Again, those are two opposite beliefs.

Obviously, all religions do not teach the same thing. Therefore, if they are opposite, one must be true and one must be false. Just being sincere doesn't make something true. For example, I could sincerely hope you have a good day today, but you might have a bad day. Just because I sincerely wanted you to have a good day didn't make it happen for you. A person can sincerely believe he or she will go to heaven, but that does not mean his or her belief is true.

Narrow-Minded

Many say Christians are narrow-minded because they believe Jesus is the only way to have a relationship with God and go to heaven. The foundation of this argument is that no one has the right to believe he or she is right and everyone else is wrong. However, most religions believe their way is the only correct way.

Other religions in the world have a set of requirements a person has to follow. They believe you have to believe a certain thing, behave in a certain way, or perform certain good acts in order to enter the afterlife. Christianity, on the other hand, is available to anyone who trusts in Jesus. Jesus does not reject anyone based on his or her gender, race, intelligence, or even past sins. He accepts anyone who will trust in Him.

KEY THEOLOGY

As we learned in our discussion about Jesus, He is God, yet He is human. He has the perfection of God (He is sinless), yet He experienced everything we experience (pain, sorrow, temptation, etc.) when He lived on earth. Because He is human, He is able to relate to our struggles; because He is God, He is powerful enough to help us overcome our struggles. We have sinned, and our sins must be punished. Jesus is the only one who ever lived and did not commit any sins. He is perfect. He is the only one who could be a legitimate sacrifice for our sins because He was not guilty of sin Himself. Jesus displayed His power by returning from the dead. No one else can make this claim. Through His return, Jesus showed us that He is more powerful than death. He also displayed that He can defeat death in us by giving us eternal life.

I know some of this theology may seem complicated, so let's look at it from a different angle. If there were another way to be saved, why would God allow His Son, Jesus, to suffer and die on the cross? He would not. He would have simply allowed Jesus to live out His life on earth, continuing to teach about goodness and love. Then, God would have taken Jesus away into heaven before He died. Further, Jesus even taught His disciples that the only way to get to heaven was through believing in Him. Jesus said, "I am the way, the truth and the life. No one comes to the Father except through me" (John 14:6).

KEY TRUTH

Jesus is the only way to heaven. Other religions do not provide a way for the forgiveness of sins. The only way we can be saved is by trusting in Jesus.

KEY VERSE

"I am the way and the truth and the life. No one comes to the Father except through me" (John 14:6).

KEY QUESTIONS

Why aren't sincere believers of other religions saved?

Is it possible to be saved without trusting in Jesus?

Why would God provide only one way to be saved?

If there were another way to be saved, do you think Jesus would have still died on the cross? Why or why not?

How would you respond to someone who says you are closed-minded if you believe Jesus is the only way to heaven?

CHAPTER 11

SECURITY OF THE BELIEVER

SECURITY OF THE BELIEVER

Once people get saved, they are secure in their salvation. In other words, a Christian does not have to worry about losing his or her salvation. However, once we get saved, we begin to realize that sometimes we still commit sins. We then become concerned God might remove His salvation from us. Some people become so worried they will try to get saved again and again, even repeating their baptism.

God does not want us to worry about whether we are still saved or not. Just as we cannot earn our salvation through good works (remember, we receive it by grace as a gift), we also cannot keep our salvation through good works. Jesus promises He and His Father will keep our salvation for us. "I give them eternal life, and they shall never perish; no one can snatch them out of my hand. My Father, who has given them to me, is greater than all; no one can snatch them out of my Father's hand. I and the Father are one" (John 10:28-29).

But what about the sins a person continues to commit? Remember, Paul continued to struggle with sin even after he was saved. In Romans 7:14-25, he wrestled with the fact that he continued to struggle with the things he did not want to do. He even went so far as to refer to himself as a wretched man. Yet according to Scripture, he never questioned his salvation, and he never "got saved" again. When Jesus Christ died on the cross, He paid for our sins—past, present, and future.

Some ask, "But what about really bad sins?" Satan loves to confuse us on this issue. He loves to convince us some sins are worse than others. We tend to measure sin: "My sin isn't as bad as his sin" or "Her sin is not as bad as mine." Satan deceives us in this way for two purposes: in order to make us judgmental of others so we will be filled with pride and self-righteousness and to isolate us in order to make us feel worse than others. The truth about sin, according to the Bible, is that all sins are really bad. All sins carry the death penalty. Recall the first part of Romans 6:23, which says, "The wages of sin is death."

Once we are saved, God changes our hearts. His Holy Spirit lives inside of us, teaches us, and helps us to do the things God wants us to do. He helps us turn away from sin. When we do sin, the Holy Spirit convicts our hearts (shows us what we have done), and we begin to feel guilty. When we love someone, we want that person to be pleased with us. Therefore, we will change our behavior (repent) in order for God to be pleased with us.

If a person does not want to live a life that is pleasing to God, then such a person does not love God and perhaps was never saved in the first place. Jesus said if we love Him, we will obey his teachings (John 14:23).

KEY THEOLOGY

Once a person is truly saved, he or she doesn't have to worry about losing salvation. Just as a person cannot earn salvation by good works, a person cannot keep his or her salvation through good works. We are secure in God's promise of salvation through Jesus' work on the cross. We are saved by grace. Grace is not earned; it is freely given—a gift.

KEY TRUTH

Once someone is truly saved, that person cannot lose his or her salvation. We are secure in the grace of God that comes from Jesus.

KEY VERSE

"It does not, therefore, depend on man's desire or effort, but on God's mercy" (Romans 9:16).

KEY QUESTIONS

If it is not possible to earn God's love, is it possible to cause God to continue to love us?

Is there anything you could do to cause God to stop loving you?

What does repentance mean?

How does the Holy Spirit help us?

What action should we take when we sin?

Have you ever had a time when you felt like God didn't love you? Why did you feel that way?

CHAPTER 12

PRIESTHOOD OF THE BELIEVER

PRIESTHOOD OF THE BELIEVER

In the Old Testament, a person needed to go to the priest for two basic reasons. First, he or she needed to go to offer sacrifices for cleansing from various disorders and sins. Second, a person needed to go in order to hear from God. When Jesus came, however, everything changed.

When Jesus died on the cross, He paid for our sins—past, present, and future. Literally, Jesus became the sacrifice for us. Therefore, we no longer have to go to the priest year after year in order to find forgiveness for any new sins we might have committed. We go straight to Jesus for our forgiveness.

The second reason for going to the priest was to hear from God. Jesus changed that as well. Jesus gave believers two very important gifts when He physically left the earth: His Word and the Holy Spirit. God's Word reveals His will and His ways to us. All we have to do is read it. The Holy Spirit guides us to understand His Word and leads us to do the things He desires for us to do. In other words, God speaks to all of us, not just the priest.

In fact, according to the Bible, we ourselves are priests! Jesus "has made us to be a kingdom and priests to serve His God and Father—to Him be glory and power for ever and ever! Amen" (Revelation 1:6, NIV). We are called to seek God daily, follow Him, help others come to know Him, and serve Him according to His will.

If that's the case, then why do we need to go to church, listen to Bible studies, and hear preaching? That's a great question. When we go to a Bible study, we get to hear what God is saying to others, and we help one another grow in the faith. Proverbs 27:17 says, "As iron sharpens iron, so one man sharpens another." Also, God has given some people a spiritual gift and a call to preach and teach to help the general group of believers grow, be challenged, and be encouraged.

KEY THEOLOGY

In the Old Testament, God set aside a certain tribe of people (the tribe of Levi) to serve as priests. He gave them specific gifts to help them carry out the work of the temple. Only the priests could carry out these specific temple functions. People had to go to the priest in order to offer sacrifices for the sins they had committed. But once Jesus died for our sins, going to the priest was no longer necessary. We do not have to offer sacrifices because Jesus became the sacrifice for us. We go to Jesus for forgiveness. God also shares His Word with all of us through the Bible and through the Holy Spirit. The Holy Spirit helps us understand God's Word. In addition, God gives every believer at least one special spiritual gift, so we can be involved in His work in the world today.

KEY TRUTH

Once we belong to God, we become priests. We are set apart to do His work here on earth and eternally in heaven. We do not need to go to a priest in order to find forgiveness of our sins or to understand God's Word. God speaks directly to us as we read His Word and seek His will.

KEY VERSE

"To him who loves us and has freed us from our sins by His blood, and has made us to be a kingdom and priests to serve his God and Father—to him be glory and power for ever and ever! Amen" (Revelation 1:5-6).

KEY QUESTIONS

In what ways are Christians priests?

Why was a priest necessary in the days before Jesus was born?

What has changed since the death and resurrection of Jesus?

What has God set you apart to do for Him?

What changes do you need to make in your life in order to be obedient to God's plan for you?

CHAPTER 13

THE CHURCH

THE CHURCH

When I was young, I often didn't want to go to church. I thought just sitting and listening was boring. Later, I discovered my problem. If I was merely sitting and listening, I was not fulfilling His purpose in my life. God has a much greater purpose for us as individuals as well as the church as a whole.

The church is very important to God and to a Christian. It's important to God because He loves the church.

Usually, when we think about the church, we think about buildings or programs. Many churches, however, do not even have a building. Some meet in schools, stores, hotels, or other available places. Other churches meet in homes. In Africa, some churches simply meet under a tree in the middle of the village. Even though these churches do not have buildings, many still are valid, fully functioning churches. According to the Bible, the church is the people of God. When the Bible speaks of the church, God may be speaking to all believers at the same time or to individual gatherings of believers.

The Bible refers to the church in three different ways: the people of God, the body of Christ, and the bride of Christ. The first is obvious. As believers, we are God's children and His people. Second, we are called the body of Christ because we carry out His work on earth today; we are His hands and feet. Third, we are called the bride of Christ because God is preparing us to be joined with Christ for all eternity in heaven.

Many churches, such as Baptist churches, believe each church will answer to God about the way it carries out the ministry to which it has been called. Therefore, each church chooses its own leaders, conducts its own ministries, and takes care of its own resources.

The church has four important purposes. One purpose is for believers to gather together to pray and worship the Lord. Another is to enable believers to fellowship with one another and encourage one another. A third purpose of the church is to teach God's Word, so we can all understand God's plans and purposes for our lives and learn how to obey Him more fully. A final purpose is to carry out the Great Commission of Jesus (Matthew 28:19-20) by teaching others—from our next-door neighbors to people of other lands and nations—about the love of God.

It is important for Christians to belong to a church and to attend regularly. Scripture says, "Let us not give up meeting together, as some are in the habit of doing, but let us encourage one another—and all the more as you see the Day approaching" (Hebrews 10:25). Paul writes that the "manifold wisdom of God should be made known" through the church (Ephesians 3:10). It is impossible to be obedient to God and grow in our faith without being actively involved in the work of the church. When a person isn't involved in church, he or she will miss the community and opportunities to help others come to know Christ. That person may also miss the support he or she will need during difficult times. God had all of these ministries in mind when He established the church.

It's important for the people of the church to get along with one another. In fact, God instructs His church to be unified so the world can believe Jesus is the Son of God (John 17:20-23). In other words, it's hard for unbelievers to believe in the love of God when they can't see love in God's church. Being unified doesn't mean we always agree about everything. It means we have the same purpose in mind: the building of the kingdom of God. Being unified means we agree together on the important matters of faith and choose to love, respect, and protect one another—even when we disagree in other areas.

KEY THEOLOGY

God established His church in order to help us grow, better understand His love, and carry out His Great Commission. Jesus died for the church. The church is not a building; it is the body of Christ. We, as His people, are the church. We belong to Jesus, not ourselves. We are also the bride of Christ. God is preparing us to be joined with Jesus for eternity in heaven. Therefore, we as the church are to keep ourselves pure and holy as we prepare for that day. God gave the church specific tasks as our work on earth: worship and glorify God, love one another, learn and grow in the faith, and share His love with the world. Through the Holy Spirit, God gave the church gifts in order to carry out His work and His purposes.

KEY TRUTH

Jesus loves the church and is committed to the church. He wants you to love the church as well. He designed us to grow and find encouragement in community.

KEY VERSE

"Husbands, love your wives, just as Christ loved the church and gave himself up for her" (Ephesians 5:25).

KEY QUESTIONS

Some Christians do not believe it is important to attend church regularly. According to the Bible, why is it important to go to church?

What does Jesus think about the church? Does He love the church?

What are the key purposes of the church?

What does the Bible mean when it states the church should be unified?

What are a few things that create division in the church?

CHAPTER 14

ORDINANCES:
BAPTISM
AND
THE LORD'S SUPPER

ORDINANCES

Most Protestant churches observe certain ordinances. An *ordinance* is a religious ritual serving as a symbol or reminder of our faith. Other churches have sacraments. A *sacrament* is an act necessary for receiving grace or salvation. The Bible teaches we do not receive grace or salvation through our own efforts or works, but only as a gift from God (Ephesians 2:8-9). Therefore, Baptist churches and many other Protestant churches do not practice sacraments, only ordinances. The two most important ordinances are baptism and the Lord's Supper (Communion).

Baptism

I was saved and baptized when I was seven years old. I remember the wonderful feeling I had immediately after my baptism. I felt very excited and renewed. Someone described her baptism experience as feeling like her sins had been washed away. The truth is baptism doesn't wash away our sins. Jesus' sacrifice washes away our sins. If the latter is the case, then why do people experience a wonderful feeling? Any time we are obedient to the Father, it causes us to feel good. It brings us joy when we know the Father is pleased with us.

Some teach that a person must be baptized in order to go to heaven. The Bible does not teach this idea. According to the Bible, we are saved by grace, not by baptism. When Jesus was dying on the cross, one of the criminals being crucified next to Him realized Jesus' identity. He asked Jesus to forgive him. Jesus said to him, "I tell you the truth, today you will be with me in paradise" (Luke 23:43). Jesus did not require the man to be baptized. The man was saved because of his faith rather than a ritual.

Remember, baptism doesn't save you; it shows the world you are saved. Baptism is similar to a wedding ring. Wearing a wedding ring doesn't automatically, magically *make* you married. You can be married even if you don't wear a ring. Wearing a ring *shows* the world you are married.

KEY THEOLOGY

Baptism is one of our first opportunities to obey God once we are saved. It is a chance for us to show the world that we now follow Jesus. Jesus commanded us to be baptized. Jesus instructed His followers to "go and make disciples of all nations, baptizing them in the name of the Father and of the Son and of the Holy Spirit" (Matthew 28:19). Jesus tells us to baptize the new believers. But why does He tell us to baptize? What does it mean?

The word *baptize* comes from the Greek word *baptizo* which means "to dip under" or "to immerse." When we are baptized (dipped under), it reminds us of what Jesus did for us—He died, was buried, and rose again (Romans 6:4-6). We die to our old, selfish ways and are raised up to live a new life for Christ. Baptism also symbolizes our sins being washed away. Baptism doesn't really wash off our sins, only Jesus can do that. It reminds us that Jesus washes our sins away.

KEY TRUTH

Baptism is a symbol of our salvation and a picture of death, burial, and resurrection. By being baptized, we share one of our very first opportunities to display our faith in Jesus publicly. We should be baptized in order to be obedient to Jesus' command. Even though Jesus commands us to be baptized, baptism does not save us. We are saved by grace through faith.

KEY VERSE

"Peter replied, 'Repent and be baptized, every one of you, in the name of Jesus Christ for the forgiveness of your sins. And you will receive the gift of the Holy Spirit'" (Acts 2:38).

The Lord's Supper

The Lord's Supper is another ordinance for believers. The Lord's Supper comes from the Passover meal—a meal the Jews began observing when Moses led the Israelites out of Egypt (Exodus 12-13). God commanded the Israelites to observe this special occasion each year with a Passover feast in order to remember God's goodness as He rescued them from slavery.

In the Gospels, Jesus gathers with His disciples in order to celebrate this important feast (Matthew 26:26-29, Mark 14:22-26, Luke 22:17-21). A significant part of the Passover feast is the cup reserved for the coming of the Messiah. During the meal, Jesus took that cup and drank it, showing He was the one God had promised would come. He is the Messiah! The Bible says He took bread, broke it, and gave it to His followers. He told them His body would be broken for them. He also took the cup and told them His blood would be poured out for them. Eating the bread and drinking the cup reminded them that everything Jesus was about to suffer was not just something happening *to Him*, it was *for them*.

In I Corinthians 11:17-34, Paul teaches we should gather with the body of believers at certain times and observe the Lord's Supper. He instructs that the ceremony should be carried out in an orderly manner and should not single out some members of the church as more important than others. He instructs us to examine our hearts carefully before taking the Lord's Supper.

Today, some churches teach that it is necessary to take the Lord's Supper in order to receive grace or forgiveness. They teach the bread literally becomes the flesh of Jesus, and the juice literally becomes the blood of Jesus. The Bible, however, teaches us to observe the Lord's Supper as a reminder rather than as a way to receive grace or salvation.

Jesus commanded us to continue to take the bread and the cup to remind us of His death for our sins. It is a symbol and a reminder of how much He loves us!

KEY THEOLOGY

The Lord's Supper was a part of the larger Passover meal, which Jesus and the Jews observed for many years. Jesus was showing His followers that He was fulfilling the portion of the meal that foretold the coming Messiah—the one who would rescue them from their sins.

Observing the Lord's Supper is not a necessary act to receive grace or forgiveness. It is a ceremony in the church serving as a symbol of Christ's sacrifice for us. Jesus told us to do it to remember Him. The bread reminds us of His body, which was broken for us, and the juice reminds us of His blood, which was poured out for us. The Lord's Supper is a symbol of His love.

KEY TRUTH

The Lord's Supper is a ceremony performed in churches as a symbol and reminder of the cost of our salvation. Jesus' body was broken, and His blood was poured out for the forgiveness of our sins.

KEY VERSE

"And when He had given thanks, He broke it and said, 'This is my body, which is for you; do this in remembrance of me.' In the same way, after supper He took the cup, saying, 'This cup is the new covenant in my blood; do this, whenever you drink it, in remembrance of me.' For whenever you eat this bread and drink this cup, you proclaim the Lord's death until he comes" (I Corinthians 11:24-26).

KEY QUESTIONS

What does the word *baptize* mean?

Does baptism save a person? Why or why not?

If a person is saved and never gets baptized, will he or she still go to heaven? Why or why not?

Why should a person be baptized?

What does baptism symbolize?

What is the purpose of the Lord's Supper?

How should we prepare ourselves for the Lord's Supper?

What do the bread and juice symbolize?

CHAPTER 15

Evangelism
and
Missions

EVANGELISM AND MISSIONS

I will never forget the moment I realized God was calling my family to move from Kentucky to Malawi, Africa, to be foreign missionaries. I was very confused. I had been obedient to other callings in my life. I shared my faith openly with others. I had even become a pastor. Wasn't that enough? Did He really want me to move so far away from family and friends, from comfort and the familiar, to tell other people about Jesus? As I prayed, God began to show me how He had prepared me for this event. He also showed me that without my obedience, some would not hear the good news of Jesus Christ. I then felt led to a verse found in Isaiah: "Then I heard the voice of the Lord saying, 'Whom shall I send, and who will go for us?' And I said, 'Here am I, send me'" (Isaiah 6:8). Was I willing to be obedient like Isaiah and answer the call of the Lord? Finally, my wife, Jill, and I realized God was calling us to go overseas to Africa to be His witnesses. So we went.

God has called all of His followers to be His missionaries. He calls some to share in their own communities, at work, and at school. He calls some to move to other communities to be His witnesses. Others, He calls to go overseas to reach the "the ends of the earth." Wherever God calls you, you can be sure that He is definitely calling you to share His love with others. When God saves us, He has a plan for us to be involved in His mission for the world. The Bible teaches, "we are God's workmanship, created in Christ Jesus to do good works, which God prepared in advance for us to do" (Ephesians 2:10).

What kind of work does God want us to do? He wants us to be involved in His mission of reaching a lost and dying world. Before Jesus went up into heaven, the last thing He taught His disciples was to "go and make disciples of all nations, baptizing them in the name of the Father and of the Son and of the Holy Spirit" (Matthew 28:19). God is calling for all of His followers to be missionaries. He wants us to start by realizing many people in our neighborhood, school, and even in our home and church do not know Jesus. God wants us to pray for them and tell them about the eternal life that comes only through Jesus. He also wants us to be involved in telling the whole world about the love of Jesus. We can do that by praying for people who do not know Jesus, by telling them the good news of Jesus, by giving money to help support missionaries, and by being willing to serve as short-term or career missionaries, pastors, or other types of ministers.

God has a plan for your life. He may want you to be a farmer, banker, doctor, factory worker, or teacher. He may be calling you to be a pastor, worship leader, youth minister, missionary, or some other worker altogether. However, He calls all of us to be faithful in spreading His good news across the globe.

KEY THEOLOGY

In the beginning of the book of Acts, God gives us His plan for evangelism and world missions. He says, "But you will receive power when the Holy Spirit comes and you will be my witnesses in Jerusalem, and in all Judea and Samaria, and to the ends of the earth" (Acts 1:8).

Many people like to debate about what happens to a person when he or she receives the Holy Spirit. According to Acts 1:8, the sign of the Holy Spirit is a person telling others about Jesus. Jesus instructs His followers to share His love with the people in their own hometown (Jerusalem), in their region (Judea and Samaria), and even to the rest of the world (the ends of the earth). This mandate includes people who are like us and people who are different from us.

The only plan for evangelism revealed in Scripture is for God's people to tell the lost about the love of Jesus. There is no other plan. In fact, in Romans, Paul wrote, "How, then, can they call on the one they have not believed in? And how can they believe in the one of whom they have not heard? And how can they hear without someone preaching to them? And how can they preach unless they are sent? As it is written, 'How beautiful are the feet of those who bring good news'" (Romans 10:14-15).

The only way the lost can hear the good news of Jesus Christ is if His followers, Christians, tell them about God's love. Then—and only then—can they respond to the message of truth.

KEY TRUTH

God commands and equips all believers to be His witnesses in this world. Our lives should be a witness to point others to Him.

KEY VERSE

"But you will receive power when the Holy Spirit comes on you; and you will be my witnesses in Jerusalem, and in all Judea and Samaria, and to the ends of the earth" (Acts 1:8).

KEY QUESTIONS

In what work is God calling all of His followers to be involved?

With whom are we supposed to share the good news?

How can you influence others in your school, work place, or community with the good news?

What changes need to occur in your life for others to see Jesus in you?

What can you do to spread the gospel to the ends of the earth?

CHAPTER 16

STEWARDSHIP

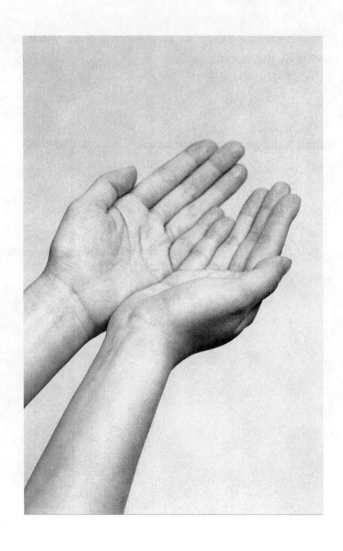

STEWARDSHIP

Out of His generosity, God has given us much. He has given us a beautiful planet on which to live. He has also given us strength and ability to make money to provide for our needs. Everything that we have comes from God's hands. The Bible teaches us, "through Him all things were made; without Him nothing was made that has been made" (John 1:3). Since He blesses us so richly, God wants us to be good stewards of all that He gives us. A *steward* is a person who takes care of something belonging to someone else. If we are going to be good stewards, we first have to recognize everything we have belongs to the Lord. He gives us all that we have in order to bless us, so we can bless others.

First, we find in Genesis 1 that God gave us the earth and told us to take care of it. He later (in Leviticus 27) taught His followers to give a tithe (which means one tenth or 10 percent) of anything the land produces as an offering to Him. Then in Malachi 3:8, God teaches that when we do not tithe, we steal from God. Jesus simply said it like this: "Give to God what is God's" (Matthew 22:21). As Paul teaches us in his letter to the church in Corinth (II Corinthians 9:7), our attitude when we give is important. He says, "God loves a cheerful giver."

Since God has given us everything we have, we should be very thankful and cheerfully return to Him what rightfully belongs to Him. We should give to our church first (the place where ministry to our family is provided). We should also look for other opportunities to bless others with our resources. We should work hard to take good care of our planet because it also belongs to God.

KEY THEOLOGY

Everything we have ultimately comes from God. I believe God instructs us to return a tenth to Him for three important reasons. First, it serves as a reminder that God is our provider. Second, it gives us an opportunity to thank God for His provision. Third, it teaches us to trust God to provide for us in the future.

Some teach that when we give, we should expect a lot of money in return. I do not find such a teaching in the Bible. I do believe, however, that God promises to bless us. He tells us He will "pour out so much blessing that you will not have room enough for it" (Malachi 3:10). Yet the Bible does not explain what those blessings look like. The blessings may include health, peace, or joy. The blessings may be encouragement or watching your church grow. They may even include having the opportunity to know the lost are being reached in other nations. But the key is when we are obedient with our resources, it shows we trust God, and we will be blessed.

God also teaches us that our attitude in giving is as important as the amount we give. Paul reminds us "whoever sows sparingly will also reap sparingly, and whoever sows generously will also reap generously. Each man should give what he has decided in his heart to give, not reluctantly or under compulsion, for God loves a cheerful giver. And God is able to make all grace abound to you, so that in all things at all times, having all that you need, you will abound in every good work" (II Corinthians 9:6-8). According to these verses, the Lord loves it when His people give out of their love and devotion to Him rather than simply to meet a requirement of His Word.

KEY TRUTH

God commands His people to return a tithe to Him. *Tithe* means tenth. When we are not obedient to God with our resources, it means we are selfish or do not trust God. God blesses us when we are faithful with our resources.

KEY VERSE

"'Bring the whole tithe into the storehouse, that there may be food in my house. Test me in this,' says the LORD Almighty, 'and see if I will not throw open the floodgates of heaven and pour out so much blessing that you will not have room enough for it'" (Malachi 3:10).

KEY QUESTIONS

What does the word *tithe* mean?

Why should a person tithe?

What are some reasons a person doesn't tithe?

Besides giving money, what are some other ways God commands us to be good stewards?

CHAPTER 17

THE END TIME

THE END TIME

Several years ago, a series of books about the end time sold by the thousands. As each new book in the series was released, fascination with the end time continued to grow. Many came to me as their pastor to ask my view about the end time. I told them that while I also enjoyed the books very much, I was not sure if that was exactly how the end time would be. I explained that before the birth of Jesus, there were many prophecies about His coming. During the time of Jesus, a group of religious scholars called the Pharisees knew the Word of God quite well. However, nearly all of these religious scholars misunderstood the coming of the Messiah and totally missed the person of Jesus. Now, if these great scholars misunderstood Jesus' first coming, then who am I to say that I totally understand everything about His second coming? However, there is one thing I know for sure. Every human being will experience an "end time." We will all face a time when we will kneel before the King of Kings and be judged based on our works or Christ's work on the cross. We should all focus on being prepared for that end time first and foremost.

With that said, we can understand quite a bit about the end time based on what the Bible teaches. Just as God had a plan for the beginning, He also has a plan for the end. He has not revealed the timing of His plan to people yet but has promised Jesus will come again. Even though many people try to predict when the end time will come, Jesus said no one knows the day or the hour (Matthew 24:36). He teaches us to always be prepared because He could come at any time (I Thessalonians 5:1-3, Luke 12:40). This truth is not something that should cause us to be afraid; instead, it should fill us with hope if we belong to Him. We can be hopeful because we know He loves us, and He promises to take us to a place where there will be no more fear, tears, pain, or sorrow. He will be there with us and will take care of us for all eternity.

KEY THEOLOGY

There is a lot of debate among Christians regarding the end time. Some believe in a rapture of believers. *Rapture* means believers are taken up from the earth and into heaven. This event is followed by seven years of tribulation, which will be a time of great struggle on the earth. Those believing in the rapture also say that after the rapture, Jesus Christ will reign on earth for one thousand years, and finally, Satan and all of his followers will suffer ultimate eternal punishment. Others believe Christians will remain on earth through the hard times and will be a part of the great battle. Still others believe the end-time Scriptures are symbolic, and God will ultimately bring things to an end according to His perfect timing. As you can see, there seems to be some disagreement among Christian leaders on this subject. Therefore, I would encourage you to read the words of Jesus in Matthew 24 along with the books of Daniel, Joel, and Revelation and discern for yourself what you believe the Bible teaches about the end time.

In the midst of the debate, however, most of us can agree on this: God, according to His wisdom, has set aside a time to bring all things to an appropriate end. We can understand from Scripture that Jesus will return. We will see Him coming in the clouds. We also know there will be a great battle in which Satan and his followers will be defeated and punished eternally. Last, we know God will make all things new. He will make a new heaven and a new earth as a place for us to live with Him for all eternity.

The key is that if we are Christ-followers, we do not have to be afraid. God has set the end time in order to punish and destroy evil. When He does this, we will no longer have to struggle with temptation or sin in our lives. We will no longer have to fear pain, suffering, or death. He will put an end to the evil of this world, and we will, at last, be able to live in perfect peace.

KEY TRUTH

At a set time, according to God's purpose and plan, He will bring this world to an appropriate end. No one knows the date or the time when the end will occur. We should always be prepared for the end time. Christ-followers do not have to fear God's plan.

KEY VERSE

"Therefore keep watch, because you do not know on what day your Lord will come. But understand this: If the owner of the house had known at what time of night the thief was coming, he would have kept watch and would not have let his house be broken into. So you also must be ready, because the Son of Man will come at an hour when you do not expect Him" (Matthew 24:42-44).

KEY QUESTIONS

Why shouldn't a Christian be frightened about the end time?

Some claim to know the date of Jesus' return. What does the Bible say regarding this claim?

Why does God plan to bring an end to this world?

How will the next world be different?

CHAPTER 18

How to Grow in Your Faith

HOW TO GROW IN YOUR FAITH

Once you become a Christian, the Bible teaches, you are born again (John 3:3). When we are born again, we start out on our Christian journey like little babies in the faith. However, God does not want us to continue as little babies; He wants us to mature in our faith. In I Corinthians 3:1-2, Paul teaches us that we begin as infants in Christ. He goes on to show (in I Corinthians 13:11) that a time should come when we begin to take steps to grow up in our faith. So how do we grow in our faith?

1. Our first important step in growing is to get involved in a Bible study group or a Sunday school class. With godly teachers who focus on the Word of God, we can learn a lot about God and His plan for our lives.

2. We should attend and join a church where God's Word is preached. Sometimes it can be difficult for a new believer to understand everything that is being preached; however, if you try to listen, you may be surprised how much you really will understand and learn.

3. Study and read God's Word for yourself. Perhaps you could begin with the Gospel of John. Then, you could read Romans. The book of Acts tells the story of the New Testament church and how it got its start, and the book of James teaches us much about how a Christian ought to live and behave. In the book of Genesis, you will find many of the Bible stories that build the foundation for our faith. Some people even like to try to read through the entire Bible in a year and there are special Bibles designed to help you. Others like to read through the New Testament in one year and the Old Testament the next year. Whatever plan you choose, just be sure you are reading God's Word. He will assist you in understanding if you will be faithful to read it.

4. Grow in your prayer life. Many people just tell God the things they want Him to do for them. That's not God's plan for your prayer life! God wants to be your friend. He wants to hear you tell Him you love Him. He wants to hear you say "thank you" for the many good things He has done for you. He wants to help you with your struggles. A formula called ACTS has helped me grow in my prayer life.

Adoration—We tell God how much we love Him and that He deserves to be worshipped. Often I will read a passage in the book of Psalms as a part of my prayer to help me express to Him the worship He deserves.

Confession—When we confess our sins to God, we not only tell Him about our sins but also agree with Him that our sins are wrong. We are able to ask Him to forgive us and give us the strength to live for Him.

Thanksgiving—This is our opportunity to thank God for all of the good things He has given us. Since we just finished confessing our sins to Him, our thanksgiving time really reminds us that we do not deserve the good things God gives us; yet, He gives them to us anyway because He loves us.

Supplication—Supplication means to ask for something. This point in our prayer is when we should ask God to help us with the things we need and help others with their struggles and problems.

5. After praying the ACTS formula, I like to take time to quiet my mind and listen to my thoughts to see if God has something He wants to say to me. Sometimes I am reminded of others I should pray for. Other times I am reminded of others I

should help or serve. Occasionally, I am convicted about a behavior in my life or attitude. Always test these thoughts to make sure they are coming from God. Make sure they are consistent with His Word. If you feel led to make a drastic change in your life, ask God to confirm it through other mature Christ-followers.

Begin serving God by telling others about Him, sharing your resources, and helping in your church. God will bless you richly as you live out your faith each day.

As you follow these five steps, you will quickly find yourself growing in your faith. As you grow in your faith, God will bless you with wisdom and knowledge. He will use you to lead others to come to know Him and help them grow in their faith as well.

KEY THEOLOGY

God wants us to mature in our faith. Most problems in the church are not due to deep or profound theological differences. Most problems are due to spiritual immaturity. Throughout the writings of Paul (Romans, I and II Corinthians, Galatians, Ephesians, Philippians, Colossians, I and II Thessalonians, I and II Timothy, Titus, and Philemon), he addressed problems in the church directly related to spiritual immaturity. Paul stated in I Corinthians 3:1 that he could not address his listeners as spiritually mature believers but as infants in Christ. Paul instructs us to become mature in our faith (Ephesians 4:11-15), so we will not be "tossed about" by every wave of false teaching that comes along.

Jesus Himself taught we are to go and make disciples (Matthew 28:19). Jesus is instructing us that our mission is not only to tell people about Him but also help them grow in the faith, so they can share His love with others. That is His plan for us. To grow in our faith means we can have a greater understanding of Jesus' love for us, love Him more, and express His love to others in a greater way.

KEY TRUTH

Christ-followers are expected to grow in their faith.

KEY VERSE

"It was he who gave some to be apostles, some to be prophets, some to be evangelists, and some to be pastors and teachers, to prepare God's people for works of service, so that the body of Christ may be built up until we all reach unity in the faith and in the knowledge of the Son of God and become mature, attaining to the whole measure of the fullness of Christ. Then we will no longer be infants, tossed back and forth by the waves, and blown here and there by every wind of teaching and by the cunning and craftiness of men in their deceitful scheming. Instead, speaking the truth in love, we will in all things grow up into him who is the Head, that is, Christ" (Ephesians 4:11–15).

KEY QUESTIONS

Why does God want you to grow in your faith?

How can attending a church affect your faith?

Describe the ACTS formula for prayer. How could this formula help you with your prayer life?

What are the five steps for spiritual growth?

What do you need to focus on as a good next step in growing in your faith?

CHAPTER 19

LIVING FOR CHRIST

*I urge you to live a life worthy of the
calling you have received.*
Ephesians 4:1

Living for Christ

When I went to college, I met many Christians. They went to church and participated in campus Christian groups. They even knew many Bible verses. I remember thinking these people had it all together. As I got to know some of them better, I found many of them *knew* Jesus, but they didn't *live* for Jesus. Their behavior and attitudes did not line up with the Word of God. Many were not honoring God with their bodies, minds, or language. I quickly found myself falling into some of the same patterns. *If God has already forgiven all of my sins,* I reasoned, *then it does not really matter what I do. He's just going to forgive me again, anyway.*

One weekend, I went on a spiritual retreat with a group of students to study the book of James. I was shocked by what I read that weekend.

> What good is it, my brothers, if a man claims to have faith but has no deeds? Can such a faith save him?
> In the same way, faith by itself, if it is not accompanied by action, is dead.
> But someone will say, "You have faith; I have deeds."
> Show me your faith without deeds, and I will show you my faith by what I do. You believe that there is one God. Good! Even the demons believe that—and shudder (James 2:14, 17-19).

> You adulterous people, don't you know that friendship with the world is hatred toward God?
> Submit yourselves, then, to God. Resist the devil, and he will flee from you. Come near to God and he will come near to you. Wash your hands, you sinners, and purify your hearts, you double-minded. Grieve, mourn and wail.

Change your laughter to mourning and your joy to gloom.
Humble yourselves before the Lord, and he will lift you up
(James 4:4, 7-10).

During the Bible study, I discovered that these words were written
to the church—to believers. God began speaking to my heart about
the way I was living my life. He challenged my behavior, and I had
no defense for my actions. I knew I was living life outside of God's
plan. I realized that what seemed like fun was going to result in bad
consequences for others and myself.

As I continued to ask questions and seek God's will for my life,
I awakened to the fact that God was calling for me to repent of
my sinful behavior and return to Him. I realized repentance had a
cost. I lost a few friends and opportunities along the way. However,
following God provided much more than I traded away. As a result of
repentance, God has blessed me with a wonderful family, many great
ministry opportunities, and peace and joy as I have journeyed with
Him.

Travel with God. Trust, follow, and obey Him. Be *sure* of what His
Word says. Live a life that pleases Him—a life consistent with His will.
God stands ready to lead you and bless you!

ABOUT THE AUTHOR

Tim Menser has served in the pastoral ministry for sixteen years, six of which were spent as a church planter. Tim has also served as an international missionary with the International Mission Board for two years as a professor at the Malawi Baptist Seminary and church planter in Lilongwe, Malawi, Africa. Tim currently is pastoring in Kentucky, where he resides with his wife, Jill, and his two sons, Zac and Will.

CPSIA information can be obtained at www.ICGtesting.com
Printed in the USA
LVOW100107150212

268638LV00002B/1/P